VOLUME
UNIVERSE'S
FINEST

D1263210

MAN/SUPERMAN

BATMAN/SUPERMAN

VOLUME 6
UNIVERSE'S FINEST

WRITTEN BY
TOM TAYLOR
PETER J. TOMASI
FRANK TIERI

PENCILS BY
ROBSON ROCHA
DOUG MAHNKE
ALEX KONAT
ELIA BONETTI
GIUSEPPE CAFARO

INKS BY
DEXTER VINES
WADE VON GRAWBADGER
NORM RAPMUND
JULIO FERREIRA
JAY LEISTEN
JAIME MENDOZA
CHRISTIAN ALAMY
JOHN LIVESAY
TOM NGUYEN
ROB HUNTER
MATT BANNING
MARK ROSLAN
ELIA BONETTI
GIUSEPPE CAFARO

COLOR BY
BLOND
WIL QUINTANA
LEE LOUGHRIDGE
WES HARTMAN

LETTERS BY
ROB LEIGH
TRAVIS LANHAM

COLLECTION COVER BY
YANICK PAQUETTE WITH
NATHAN FAIRBAIRN

SUPERMAN CREATED BY
JERRY SIEGEL & JOE SHUSTER
SUPERGIRL BASED ON
THE CHARACTERS CREATED BY
JERRY SIEGEL & JOE SHUSTER
BY SPECIAL ARRANGEMENT WITH
THE JERRY SIEGEL FAMILY

BATMAN CREATED BY
BOB KANE WITH **BILL FINGER**

ANDREW MARINO Assistant Editor – Original Series
DAVID WOHL, MARIE JAVINS Editors – Original Series
JEB WOODARD Group Editor – Collected Editions
LIZ ERICKSON Editor – Collected Edition
STEVE COOK Design Director – Books
DAMIAN RYLAND Publication Design

BOB HARRAS Senior VP – Editor-in-Chief, DC Comics

DIANE NELSON President
DAN DiDIO Publisher
JIM LEE Publisher
GEOFF JOHNS President & Chief Creative Officer
AMIT DESAI Executive VP – Business & Marketing Strategy, Direct to Consumer & Global Franchise Management
SAM ADES Senior VP – Direct to Consumer
BOBBIE CHASE VP – Talent Development
MARK CHIARELLO Senior VP – Art, Design & Collected Editions
JOHN CUNNINGHAM Senior VP – Sales & Trade Marketing
ANNE DePIES Senior VP – Business Strategy, Finance & Administration
DON FALLETTI VP – Manufacturing Operations
LAWRENCE GANEM VP – Editorial Administration & Talent Relations
ALISON GILL Senior VP – Manufacturing & Operations
HANK KANALZ Senior VP – Editorial Strategy & Administration
JAY KOGAN VP – Legal Affairs
THOMAS LOFTUS VP – Business Affairs
JACK MAHAN VP – Business Affairs
NICK J. NAPOLITANO VP – Manufacturing Administration
EDDIE SCANNELL VP – Consumer Marketing
COURTNEY SIMMONS Senior VP – Publicity & Communications
JIM (SKI) SOKOLOWSKI VP – Comic Book Specialty Sales & Trade Marketing
NANCY SPEARS VP – Mass, Book, Digital Sales & Trade Marketing

BATMAN/SUPERMAN VOLUME 6: UNIVERSE'S FINEST

Published by DC Comics. Compilation, BATMAN/SUPERMAN 33, 34, BATMAN/SUPERMAN ANNUAL 3 and all new material
Copyright © 2017 DC Comics. All Rights Reserved. Originally published in single magazine form in BATMAN/SUPERMAN 28-32.
Copyright © 2016 DC Comics. All Rights Reserved. All characters, their distinctive likenesses and related elements featured in this
publication are trademarks of DC Comics. The stories, characters and incidents featured in this publication are entirely fictional.
DC Comics does not read or accept unsolicited submissions of ideas, stories or artwork.

DC Comics, 2900 West Alameda Ave., Burbank, CA 91505
Printed by LSC Communications, Salem, VA. 7/14/17. First Printing.
ISBN: 978-1-4012-7156-5

Library of Congress Cataloging-in-Publication Data is available.

UNIVERSE'S FINEST

Writer: **TOM TAYLOR** Pencils: **ROBSON ROCHA**
Inks: **DEXTER VINES, WADE von GRAWBADGER, NORM RAPMUND** Colors: **BLOND** Letters: **ROB LEIGH**

"--AND MEET ME AT THE CAVE."

MASTER WAYNE.

HE'S HERE, SIR.

YOU STOPPED FOR TEA?

I DIDN'T EVEN SEE ALFRED GIVE IT TO ME.

IT'S HIS SUPERPOWER.

I DELIVERED CLAYFACE. THE ARKHAM STAFF WERE VERY GRATEFUL.

I'D PREFER THEY WERE COMPETENT.

THERE'S SOMETHING YOU...THERE'S SOMETHING BATMAN NEEDS TO SEE.

I'LL PREPARE YOUR SUIT, SIR.

I'M GUESSING, ALFRED, GIVEN RECENT EVENTS, WHATEVER SUPERMAN WANTS TO SHOW ME IS ON THE MOON.

I'LL PREPARE YOUR OTHER SUIT, SIR.

WHAT IS IT?

THERE'S SOMETHING OUTSIDE.

IT'S OVERRIDING THE DEFENSES!

NO, IT ISN'T.

WHAT?

YOU EXPECT ME TO BELIEVE YOU DON'T HAVE ANY LONG-RANGE OR SHORT-RANGE SENSORS? YOU KNEW THIS WAS COMING.

YOUR DAUGHTER. HOW DID YOU KNOW WHERE TO FIND HER?

THERE IS NO TIME FOR THESE QUESTIONS. SOMETHING IS DOCKING WITH THE SHIP.

YOUR SHIP.

IT RUNS ON STARLIGHT.

YOU MEAN SUNLIGHT. EVERYTHING IS POWERED BY THE SUN. YOU SAID YOUR FAMILY HARNESSED IT. THE SUN IN SCORCH SPACE.

MYLARA SUSPECTED SOMETHING. DIDN'T SHE?

AND, AS YOU ALWAYS FEARED, HER CURIOSITY LED HER INTO TROUBLE.

NOT ENTIRELY, BUT CLOSE ENOUGH. I DON'T KNOW HOW YOU FIT A BRAIN LIKE THAT IN SUCH A TINY HEAD.

IT DOESN'T MATTER.

YOU!!

HE'S GONE!

WHERE IS HE?!

I DON'T KNOW. IT'S KIND OF HARD TO SEE WITHOUT A FACE!!

FIND HIM!!

CALM DOWN! HE'S IN HERE SOMEWHERE. IT'S NOT LIKE HE CAN STEP OUT--

THE AIRLOCK.

MY SHIP.

The Lost KRYPTONIAN

Writer: **TOM TAYLOR** Art: **ROBSON ROCHA & JÚLIO FERREIRA**
Colors: **BLOND** Letters: **ROB LEIGH** Cover: **YANICK PAQUETTE**
Editor: **DAVID WOHL** Group Editor: **EDDIE BERGANZA**

WE HAVE SUPERMAN.

SO, THERE'S ONLY ONE LOOSE END LEFT. ONE I ARRANGED FOR YOU TO TAKE CARE OF, LOBO.

YOU? *YOU'RE* FINANCING THIS?

I'M NOT FINANCING ANYTHING WITHOUT A BODY.

YOU'LL GET ONE. BATMAN TOOK MY FACE OFF. I'D ALMOST TAKE HIM OUT FOR FREE.

HOW? HE COULD BE ANYWHERE.

HE TOOK *MY* SHIP. I HAVE A LOCATOR ON IT. I DEAL WITH CRIMINALS MOST DAYS. YOU DON'T GET INTO MY LINE OF WORK AND TRUST PEOPLE NOT TO STEAL YOUR STUFF.

BATMAN. IF YOU SCRATCH MY SHIP, I WILL TAKE IT OUT ON YOU.

THERE'S NOWHERE TO HIDE OUT THERE.

"MEET THE COLD VACUUM OF SPACE."

STUPID HUMAN. TAKE MY SHIP. TAKE MY FINGER. TAKE OFF MY FACE.

I SHOULD HAVE THOUGHT OF A MORE INVENTIVELY PAINFUL WAY TO KILL YOU, YOU CAPE-WEARING &%$#.

HERE.

Unf!

Unf?

DEAD PEOPLE DON'T SAY "*Unf.*"

JUST...I NEED TO UNDERSTAND WHY.

I NEEDED HER COMPASSION TO BRING SUPERMAN TO SCORCH SPACE, BUT SHE WAS ALWAYS TOO CURIOUS, AND SHE WORKED OUT MY INVOLVEMENT. IF SHE'D TOLD SUPERMAN, WELL, IT COULD HAVE BEEN A PROBLEM.

WHY DID YOUR DAUGHTER HAVE TO DIE?

SHE WASN'T SUPPOSED TO LEAVE A MESSAGE FOR BOTH OF YOU.

SHE WAS YOUR DAUGHTER.

YES. AND SHE WAS A CREDIT TO THIS FAMILY, FOR A WHILE.

I THINK YOUR MISTAKE WAS THINKING WE'RE LIKE YOU. I ATE HER THREE SMALLER SIBLINGS WHILE THEY WERE STILL IN THE NEST.

FOR THE POWER I'M REAPING, A FEW LIVES ARE NOTHING.

NO LIFE IS NOTHING.

YOURS IS.

EARTH. LATER.

Previously,
in SUPERMAN #51...

His never-ending battles have finally taken their toll on the Last Son of Krypton. After repeated exposure to Kryptonite and the fire pits of Apokolips, as well as encounters with the Kryptonian sun god, Rao, Superman faces an irrefutable diagnosis: he is dying.

With the time he has left, Superman chooses to say good-bye to those closest to him, and seeks to prepare the people of Earth for a future without their greatest hero. But even though he's getting sicker, there's always a job for Superman.

Halfway around the world in China, his residual solar energy flares become the source of mysterious tests conducted by Dr. Omen. And, closer to home, after being struck by a strange energy blast, an escaped convict begins manifesting unusual powers and believes himself to be none other than the Man of Steel...

GOTHAM.

The Final Days of SUPERMAN Part 2: DARK DISCOVERY

story and words: **PETER J. TOMASI** penciller: **DOUG MAHNKE** inker: **JAIME MENDOZA**
colors: **WIL QUINTANA** letters: **ROB LEIGH** cover: **YANICK PAQUETTE & NATHAN FAIRBAIRN**
assistant editor: **ANDREW MARINO** group editor: **EDDIE BERGANZA**

THE FIRE PITS OF APOKOLIPS.

BATTLE WITH RAO.

A.R.G.U.S. KRYPTONITE CHAMBER...

...A PERFECT STORM, CLARK...

THAT I'VE FOUND MYSELF SMACK-DAB IN THE MIDDLE OF.

YOUR FORTRESS TESTS--DID YOU RUN--

TERMINAL.

PLAIN AND SIMPLE.

NOTHING'S SIMPLE, CLARK.

I BROUGHT DAMIAN BACK FROM THE DARK, DAMN IT...

...AND YOU'RE *STILL* HERE WITH US.

WITH EVERYTHING WE HAVE AT OUR DISPOSAL--

LOOK, IF I THOUGHT THERE WAS A CHANCE TO FIX THIS I'D TAKE IT, BUT THERE'S NOT.

THIS... *KRYPTONITE MALIGNANCY* EATING AWAY AT ME... IS DIFFERENT.

WITH ALL THE CRAZY BATTLES WE'VE FOUGHT-- WE SHOULD HAVE DIED A THOUSAND TIMES OVER.

I'VE RESIGNED MYSELF TO WHAT'S COMING.

AND I'M NOT HERE IN SEARCH OF HOPE OR SYMPATHY, BRUCE.

I'M HERE BECAUSE I NEED YOU TO FIND SOMEONE.

CHŌU XIĒ!

WHY ARE WE THE TARGET?

NO IDEA!

CHŌU XIĒ!

THEY KEEP REPEATING THE SAME WORDS.

CHŌU XIĒ!

THANKS, I KIND OF PICKED UP ON THAT.

CHŌU XIĒ!

NORTHERN DIALECT...

CHŌU XIĒ!

CHŌU XIĒ!

CHŌU XIĒ!

MANDARIN.

BAMMM

THEY'RE A LONG WAY FROM HOME.

AND WE NEED TO FIND OUT WHY, SO LET'S--

Previously,
in ACTION COMICS #51
and SUPERMAN/WONDER WOMAN #28...

Shocked to find Supergirl voluntarily imprisoned in a secret D.E.O. laboratory, Superman takes Kara to the Fortress of Solitude where she will take on the mantle of Earth's sole Kryptonian protector. They are tracked there by a heartbroken Wonder Woman, who has come to hear about Clark's condition directly.

Meanwhile, the unstable Superman imposter attempts to go to work at the *Daily Planet*, causing havoc when he's unable to control his temper or the scorching energy emanating from his body. Steve Trevor and A.R.G.U.S. are able to contain this false Superman, but only after three security guards are left dead in his wake.

Back at A.R.G.U.S. headquarters, Clark, Diana and Steve work to discover the connection between Superman and his impersonator. They realize his powers are similar to the solar flare energy the Man of Steel used to defeat Ulysses, but not before the imposter manifests a solar flare strong enough to allow him to break out of his containment cell...

HOW COULD HE NOT LEAVE A TRAIL AFTER BREAKING OUT OF A.R.G.U.S.?

IT DOESN'T MATTER, A WAYNETECH SATELLITE PICKED UP YOUR *SOLAR FLARE ENERGY SIGNATURE*, AND BASED ON EVERYTHING WE NOW KNOW, IT CAN ONLY BE HIM.

WHEN I CONFRONTED HIM AT THE FACILITY, THERE WAS SO MUCH EMOTION IN HIS VOICE...

I *DIDN'T* NEED MY LASSO TO KNOW HE BELIEVED EVERY WORD HE SAID, BATMAN.

FOR ALL INTENTS AND PURPOSES, HE *TRULY* THINKS HE'S *SUPERMAN*.

OUR JOB'S TO FIND HIM AND *DISSUADE* HIM OF THAT FACT.

HOW MUCH FARTHER?

ABOUT A HUNDRED MILES.

HOW ARE YOU HOLDING UP, CLARK?

NOW THAT I'M *NOT* THREE MILES UNDERGROUND AWAY FROM THE SUN-- BETTER, ACTUALLY. NOT AS WEAK AT THE MOMENT.

GOOD TO HEAR, AND I'M HAPPY TO SEE YOU BOTH GOT THINGS FIGURED OUT.

DID *BATMAN* JUST USE THE WORD "*HAPPY*"?

DON'T LISTEN TO DIANA. I APPRECIATE YOU COMING OUT WITH US TO HELP ME STOP THIS...*THING.*

THAT'S WHAT *FRIENDS* ARE FOR, CLARK.

The Final Days of
SUPERMAN Part 5:
OMEN OF DEAT

story and words: **PETER J. TOMASI** penciller: **DOUG MAHNKE**
inkers: **JAIME MENDOZA, CHRISTIAN ALAMY, LIVESAY & TOM NGUYEN**
colors: **WIL QUINTANA** letters: **ROB LEIGH**
cover: **YANICK PAQUETTE & NATHAN FAIRBAIRN**
assistant editor: **ANDREW MARINO** group editor: **EDDIE BERGANZA**

ARRGH

YAAHH

--SOME KIND OF FORCE FIELD-- ALL AROUND US--

NRGGH

--I HEAR SOMETHING-- HIGH-RANGE VOCAL DISTORTION--

WMMMMMM

--PLANE'S BEING PUSHED DOWN--

--CAN'T EJECT--

FRAAH

KOOM

WE'RE NOT GOING TO HAVE TO LOOK FAR TO FIND WHO DID THIS.

HELLO...

WE HAVE QUESTIONS!

HGNN

DON'T

EXPECT

ANSWERS!

NARGH

SKRAKK

KRAK RAK KRAK KRAK KRAK

ZZRAKK

YETI, SHOW THE AMERICAN WHAT WE THINK OF HIS TEMERITY!

GRRGGH

BRAGHH

AND YOUR LACK OF HOSPITALITY!

MY VOCAL DISTORTION CAN ONLY TEMPORARILY PARALYZE HER, GHOST FOX!

THAT'S WHY IT'S TIME FOR--

--THE JADE LION TO MAKE HER ACQUAINTANCE!

GRRFF

KOOM

NNGG

RRROOAAAR

IF PUTTING YOU DOWN HARD--

--IS THE ONLY WAY--

--WE'RE GOING TO GET YOU TO LISTEN--

--THEN THE HARD WAY--

SHUNK

SHUNK

--IT IS.

Hmm?

BZZT

TROUBLE WITH YOUR HEAT VISION, SUPERMAN?

JUST A SIMPLE REDIRECTION OF ENERGY...

--CONTROL YOUR--

--YOUR RAGE, MY FRIEND--

GAARHH

WHAMM

THE MEDALLION!

HOLD STILL, CREATURE--

--I THINK YOU--

--DROPPED SOMETHING!

RRRNN

SKKTS

GRRR?

NOT JUST MUSIC SOOTHES THE SAVAGE BREAST, huh?

NNN

...SAVED MY LIFE...

THAT... PENDANT KEEPS HIS BERSERKER RAGE... AT BAY.

YEAH, WE KINDA NOTICED.

Hmm?

"...WE WILL ESCORT YOU THERE OURSELVES."

IT IS MY PLEASURE TO WELCOME *SUPER-FUNCTIONARIES* TO MY HUMBLE LABORATORY.

NOTHING HUMBLE ABOUT THIS PLACE, *DR. OMEN.*

I AM HAPPY TO HEAR THE *AUGUST GENERAL IN IRON* KNOWS OF ME--BUT I MUST CONFESS, I AM QUITE PERTURBED TO SEE AMERICAN IMPERIALISTS STANDING BEFORE ME WITH A CLEAR AND PRESENT VIEW OF MANY OF CHINA'S GREATEST SECRETS.

THESE JUSTICE LEAGUE MEMBERS ARE UNDER THE IMPRESSION THAT--

YOU'VE BEEN GATHERING AND MANIPULATING RESIDUAL STREAMS OF SUPERMAN'S COALESCED SOLAR SUPER-FLARE

"WHAT ARE WE WAITING FOR?

LET'S GET AFTER HIM!

THIS IS A CHINESE MATTER, SUPERMAN.

WHILE HE IS WITHIN OUR BORDERS, THE GREAT TEN WILL HUNT HIM DOWN.

UNLESS YOU PREFER TO CREATE AN INTERNATIONAL INCIDENT BETWEEN OUR TWO COUNTRIES?

WHAT I PREFER IS TO KEEP A CLEAR LINE OF COMMUNICATION OPEN BETWEEN US WITHOUT ANY ANIMOSITY OR SECRECY REGARDING THIS SITUATION.

AS DO WE.

GOOD.

BECAUSE OUR FOCUS HAS TO BE ON FINDING THE ENERGY CREATURE REPLICATING ME.

GHOST FOX WILL ESCORT YOU ALL BACK TO THE BORDER.

THAT'S NOT NECESSARY.

I HAVE YOUR WORD YOU WILL LEAVE CHINESE AIRSPACE IMMEDIATELY.

YES.

THEN THAT IS GOOD ENOUGH FOR ME.

BEST OF LUCK IN YOUR SEARCH.

YOU, TOO.

TAKATAK
TAK TAK
TAK

TAP TAP
TAP

WHAT THE HELL... HE'S BACK...

...HOW DID HE ESCAPE FROM A.R.G.U.S.?

PLAY THIS COOL, LOIS...DON'T GET HIM AGITATED....

...AFTER WHAT HE DID AT THE PLANET...

...TO GET ALONG... JUST GO ALONG...

A note on
BATMAN/SUPERMAN #33, ANNUAL #3 and #34...

These issues were created specifically for inclusion in this collected edition.
They take place years before the "Final Days of Superman" story line, which
begins in ACTION COMICS #51 and continues in this volume with BATMAN/
SUPERMAN #31.

NOW THEN... WHAT DO YOU GUYS WANT?

WELL, HELLO TO YOU TOO, AMYGDALA.

SORRY, CROC...BEEN *ONE* OF THOSE NIGHTS.

BROKE UP THREE FIGHTS, GOT SHOT, STABBED, FREEZE-RAYED AND URINATED ON...AND IT AIN'T EVEN EIGHT YET.

ANYWAY, YA GOT TONIGHT'S PASSWORD?

"@#$% THE JUSTICE LEAGUE."

GO AHEAD... AND DO ME A FAVOR AND TELL SOMEBODY IN THERE WE NEED A NEW DOOR.

AGAIN.

THAT'S THE IDEA. IT'S ALL VERY HUSH HUSH. *INVITE* ONLY.

WE DON'T WANT ANY BOY SCOUTS SHOWIN' UP, RUININ' EVERYONE'S GOOD TIME, YA KNOW?

"I MEAN, WHERE ELSE CAN YA FIND THE FLASH ROGUES THROWIN' A FEW BACK."

I ASKED FOR EXTRA ICE.

"WHILE A DEAD GUY MAKES LIKE FRIGGIN' JOHN TRAVOLTA?"

ME SOLOMON GRUNDY LIKE THIS SONG.

"AND YEAH, SOMETIMES THINGS CAN GET A BIT NASTY IN HERE LIKE AMYGDALA SAID BUT MOSTLY WE GET ALONG IN HERE PRETTY OKAY.

"HELL, EVEN CAT AND FISH PEOPLE."

SO YEAH. LIVEWIRE'S RIGHT. SUPERMAN OVER BATMAN ANY DAY OF THE WEEK.

ANYBODY WHO'S EVER FOUGHT HIM WOULD KNOW.

OH YEAH? AND HAVE YA EVER ACTUALLY FOUGHT BATMAN, TOUGH GUY?

NOPE. DON'T NEED TO.

LIKE SHE SAID, A GOOF IN GOOFY UNDERWEAR.

GUY'S GOT NO POWERS.

EXACTLY.

I MEAN, REALLY...SO WHAT'S HE GONNA DO? HIT ME WITH A BATARANG?

OR BETTER YET...SIC ROBIN HIS BOY-TOY WONDER ON ME?

OOOOOOH, I'M SOOO SCARED.

PLEASE. BATMAN'S A JOKE.

CLEARLY...

SO I'M A FOOL, *HUH?* AND WHAT DOES THAT MAKE YOU?

THE GUY WHO ONLY REALLY MADE A NAME FOR HIMSELF BY BEATING BATMAN, THAT'S WHO. SO GEE, I WONDER WHICH SIDE OF THIS LITTLE DEBATE YOU ARE GONNA BE ON?

THERE IS NO DEBATE HERE. YOU'VE *NEVER* FOUGHT BATMAN. YOU KNOW *NOTHING* ABOUT HIM OR WHAT IT TAKES TO DEFEAT HIM.

I KNOW YOU'RE *NOT* SUCH A BIG DEAL ANYMORE IF PEOPLE START THINKING BATMAN AIN'T SO TOUGH TO BEAT.

YOU CAN FIND OUT WHAT KIND OF "BIG DEAL" I AM ANYTIME YOU'D LIKE.

CRISS CROSS PART 2

FRANK TIERI: writer **ALEX KONAT:** penciller, odd pages **MATT BANNING & MARK ROSLAN:** inks, odd pages
ELIA BONETTI: pencils & inks, even pages **LEE LOUGHRIDGE:** colors **TRAVIS LANHAM:** letters

BRRG

WHAT DO YOU WANT?

Major Disaster

...BETTING SUPERMAN...

...BATMAN HAS NO CHANCE AGAINST THOSE GUYS. GONNA GET KILLED...

...SCREW THAT, BETTIN' BATMAN...

...BETTER ODDS...

...LONGSHOT, I TELL YA. BUT HEY, IT'S YOUR MONEY...

...WHY THE BOOKIES CALLIN' IT "CRISS CROSS" ANYWAY...

OH CRAP...

IT'S HIM!

WHAM

YOU KNOW, I STAND CORRECTED.

SSSSS

YOU CAME AS ADVERTISED. MORE POWERS THAN I CAN EVEN KEEP TRACK OF. STILL...

EVEN YOU NEED TO BREATHE.

KRSSSH

ACK!

HA! THOUGHT YOU HAD ME FOR A SEC THERE, DIDN'T YOU?

GUESS THE BAD NEWS IS MY "ATOMIC SKULL" ISN'T THAT EASY TO CRACK AFTER ALL.

WELL, CLAYFACE...

DON'T REALLY KNOW WHAT THIS WAS ALL ABOUT.

DON'T MUCH CARE.

KRSSSH

EXCEPT THAT WE'RE DONE HERE.

NAH...

CRACK

CROC, GET OVER HERE--

HE'S FREEZING ME AGAIN!

DON'T WORRY, I GOT YER BACK, PAL. BAT ROGUES STICK TOGETHER, RIGHT?

IN FACT... WHAT'S THE NAME OF THAT CHICK SUPER STOOGE OVER HERE IS ALWAYS HANGIN' AROUND WITH? *LOIS LANE,* RIGHT?

I SAY YOU AND ME PAY HER A VISIT WHEN THIS IS ALL OVER WITH.

OKAY.

I'VE HAD JUST ABOUT *ENOUGH.*

UHHH...

ALL SYSTEMS FRIED...

AND THEY'RE ALREADY HERE.

NEW MODIFICATIONS BETTER WORK...

I'M GOOD AS DEAD OTHERWISE.

CLANK

CLANK

CLANK

SHOULD'VE THOUGHT OF THIS BEFORE.

RRRRIP

THING IS, YOU JUST CAN'T FIND A GOOD TELEPHONE BOOTH ANYMORE.

AND BELIEVE ME, I'VE TRIED.

ZZZAP

OKAY, CROC...

THIS IS OVER.

OH, NOT YET IT AIN'T.

HEY!

ZZZZAP

MAYBE YOU DIDN'T HEAR ME THE FIRST TIME.

YA LOST.

YEAH, LIKE WE DIDN'T TAKE CARE OF THE STOOGE OF STEEL? BLOW IT OUT YER CAN, *DISASTER*.

THIS IS A *DRAW* AT BEST.

DRAWS ARE LIKE KISSING YOUR SISTER. AND I DON'T KNOW ABOUT YOU GUYS, BUT IT AIN'T LIKE THAT IN MY FAMILY.

DISASTER DON'T DO DRAWS, IN OTHER WORDS.

AND I DON'T DO PISSING CONTESTS.

I WAS JUST HERE TO BEAT *SUPERMAN*, BOYS.

SO NOW THAT I'VE DONE THAT, IF YOU'LL EXCUSE ME...

GOOD. LET THE GREEN BEAN GO.

ONE LESS *LOSER* WE GOTTA WORRY ABOUT.

ME BIZARRO NOT GIVE YOU FROSTY THE SNOWMAN FACE NOW, CROCODILE MAN. HA! HA! HA...

EH?

SNIF! SNIF!

ME BIZARRO NOT SMELL SOMETHING BURNING...

YA KNOW WHERE OUR MISTAKE WAS?

WE GOT COCKY. WALKIN' INTO THAT BAR LIKE THAT. GETTIN' INVOLVED IN SOME STUPID ARGUMENT ABOUT WHOSE ROGUES GALLERY IS TOUGHER...

I MEAN, WHO CARES, RIGHT?

KNOW WHERE MY MISTAKE WAS?

I NEVER SHOULD'VE TEAMED UP WITH *YOU*.

NOW SHUT UP...I'D LIKE TO SPEND MY LAST FEW MINUTES OF FREEDOM IN PEACE.

SO...

THAT LEX IS SOMETHING ELSE, HUH?

THAT'S ONE WAY TO PUT IT, YEAH. YOU'RE LUCKY YOU DON'T HAVE TO DEAL WITH HIM EVERY DAY LIKE I DO.

STILL... IT'S NOT LIKE HE'S THE JOKER.

ARE YOU SERIOUSLY COMPARING LEX TO THE JOKER? LEX IS A CRIMINAL MASTERMIND WITH VAST RESOURCES...

THE JOKER'S JUST A LUNATIC.

OH REALLY? YOU TRY DEALING WITH THAT "JUST A LUNATIC" SOMETIME.

The End!

FREDDIE E.
WILLIAMS II

"Batman is getting a brand-new voice."
– USA TODAY

"A great showcase for the new team as well as offering a taste of the new flavor they'll be bringing to Gotham City." **– IGN**

DC UNIVERSE REBIRTH
BATMAN

VOL. 1: I AM GOTHAM
TOM KING
with DAVID FINCH

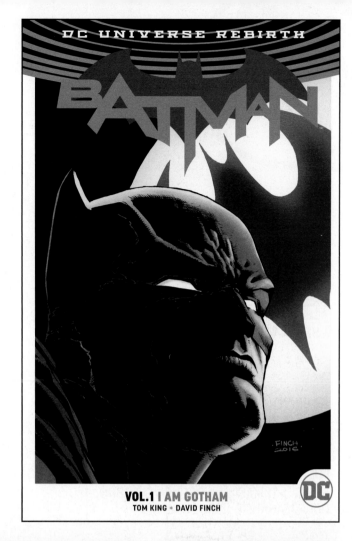

VOL.1 I AM GOTHAM
TOM KING * DAVID FINCH

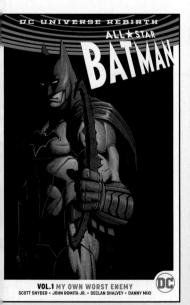

VOL.1 MY OWN WORST ENEMY
SCOTT SNYDER * JOHN ROMITA JR. * DECLAN SHALVEY * DANNY MIKI

**ALL-STAR BATMAN VOL. 1:
MY OWN WORST ENEMY**

VOL.1 BETTER THAN BATMAN
TIM SEELEY * JAVIER FERNÁNDEZ * CHRIS SOTOMAYOR

**NIGHTWING VOL. 1:
BETTER THAN BATMAN**

VOL.1 RISE OF THE BATMEN
JAMES TYNION IV * EDDY BARROWS * ALVARO MARTINEZ * EBER FERREIRA * RAÚL FERNÁNDEZ

**DETECTIVE COMICS VOL. 1:
RISE OF THE BATMEN**

Get more DC graphic novels wherever comics and books are sold!

"That gorgeous spectacle is an undeniable part of Superman's appeal, but the family dynamics are what make it such an engaging read."
— **A.V. CLUB**

"Head and shoulders above the rest."
— **NEWSARAMA**

DC UNIVERSE REBIRTH

SUPERMAN

VOL. 1: SON OF SUPERMAN

PETER J. TOMASI with PATRICK GLEASON, DOUG MAHNKE & JORGE JIMENEZ

VOL. 1 SON OF SUPERMAN
PETER J. TOMASI ∗ PATRICK GLEASON ∗ DOUG MAHNKE ∗ JORGE JIMENEZ ∗ MICK GRAY

VOL. 1 REIGN OF THE SUPERMEN
STEVE ORLANDO ∗ BRIAN CHING ∗ MIKE ATIYEH

**SUPERGIRL VOL. 1:
REIGN OF THE SUPERMEN**

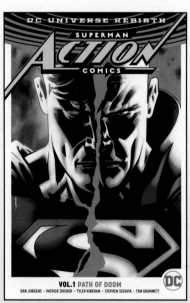

VOL. 1 PATH OF DOOM
DAN JURGENS ∗ PATRICK ZIRCHER ∗ TYLER KIRKHAM ∗ STEPHEN SEGOVIA ∗ TOM GRUMMETT

**ACTION COMICS VOL. 1:
PATH OF DOOM**

VOL. 1 I AM GOTHAM
TOM KING ∗ DAVID FINCH

**BATMAN VOL. 1:
I AM GOTHAM**

Get more DC graphic novels wherever comics and books are sold!